Romano-British coarse pottery: a student's guide

Third Edition

Edited by
Graham Webster

1976

Research Report 6   Council for British Archaeology

1st edition 1964
2nd edition 1969
3rd edition 1976

© Council for British Archaeology 1976

7 Marylebone Road, London NW1 5HA

ISBN 0 900312 38 6

Contents

Printed ⓐⓣ Tomes of Leamington

Foreword

These notes attempt to establish a consistent method of describing and illustrating Romano-British coarse pottery for which there have been and still are many different terms used for the same thing. This modest venture should be accepted as a move towards the clarification of the terms in use for types of fabric, decoration and vessel of the period, rather than any desire to impose a rigid system to which all are expected to conform. It should be helpful to amateur and professional alike in classifying and publishing the large quantity of pottery which most excavations of this period inevitably produce.

The task of compiling and publishing these notes has been that of the Iron Age and Roman Research Committee of the CBA but there has also been close collaboration with many excavators having wide experience in handling and publishing Romano-British coarse pottery. In particular the Committee acknowledges the generous help received from Miss M Bimson, the late Dr Philip Corder, Professor Sheppard Frere, Professor C F C Hawkes, Mr B R Hartley, the late Professor Sir Ian Richmond, and Mr J P Gillam, who in addition has provided many illustrations. In a work with so many hands it has sometimes been difficult to find a common area of agreement without avoiding vagueness and inconsistency. I should be grateful for further comments and suggestions which would enable improvements to be made in any subsequent edition.

1964

GRAHAM WEBSTER
Secretary of the Iron Age and
Roman Research Committee

The publication of a second edition has enabled me to incorporate several suggestions made by my colleagues and correspondents. An attempt has also been made to bring the list of stratified groups up-to-date.

1969

GRAHAM WEBSTER

This third edition must be regarded as an interim until a much expanded one can be prepared with greater objectivity in describing fabrics and a section on thin-section analysis. The additions and alterations made in this edition reflect the results of research in recent years.

1975

GRAHAM WEBSTER

Introduction

Throughout much of the prehistoric period the pottery industry was domestic, and it displays much conservatism in manufacture and design. The mass-production of pottery in specialized centres began in general only towards the end of the Iron Age, and its full development was one of the results of the Roman conquest. In the early years of Roman Britain, and indeed for some 40 years before this, much of the better pottery was imported from centres in Gaul or further afield, and sites of this date display a remarkable variety of imports and their copies in many different fabrics. Later in the first century, however, local potters began to capture the market, and by the second century there is much uniformity of overall style. Nevertheless, in detail differences of shape and/or fabric continue to occur and the study of these is basic to any attempt to use pottery for dating purposes.

The dating of archaeological sites, indeed, depends very largely on the study of pottery. In the Roman Empire pottery can often be very closely dated from its occurrence in contexts for which there is independent dating evidence.

The occurrence of coins in sufficient numbers can, when correctly interpreted, provide an independent check on date, but above all the stratification in forts, whose sequence can be related by the evidence of ancient historians or by inscriptions to the events of history, provides invaluable testimony. This evidence is all the more useful since the pottery found often includes samian imported from the continent. The decoration on samian, with its changing styles attributable to the phases of the working life of individual potters, thus acquires an additional and almost independent value as a date-scale for the local wares found in association.

The local pottery of Roman Britain was made at a great number of places where suitable clay and fuel were obtainable, and consists of a wide variety of fabrics both coarse and fine. The shapes and fabric of the vessels produced were not static, but, like present-day pottery or china, underwent modification with the passage of time and changes of fashion. If these changes can be dated, the sherds found in various deposits in an excavation can be used as a time-scale. Caution is needed in any attempt of this kind, however, since such sequence of shape and fabric cannot be assumed to possess universal validity. Some potters in Roman Britain had large outputs, others small; some traded their wares over large distances, the products of others had only a local distribution. And it is not always the smaller potters whose products were confined to a local distribution.

In the study of pottery from a site, parallels (that is, vessels of similar shape and fabric) have to be sought among published examples from dated contexts elsewhere. But these parallels will not be completely valid unless they are products of the same factory. Thus in some cases only parallels from very local sites can be cited; in others they can be obtained from sites much further away. Only close acquaintance with actual fabrics built up on experience can help in the elucidation of this sort of problem. A more general similarity of form and fabric is a much less certain guide. Much of the current published dating of Romano-British coarse pottery is erroneous because of the neglect of these principles, and often the error is cumulative when badly or wrongly dated vessels have themselves been quoted in the quest for a date for sherds not really comparable. In some cases, moreover, close dating may not be possible.

For this reason the study of potters' kilns and their products is important. At the kiln site, groups of vessels can be identified as the products of single factories, even if the close dating of these products has to depend on the discovery of examples in dated contexts elsewhere. The kilns themselves, however, when properly excavated, have much to teach us about the methods and organization of the industry. It is for this reason that offprints of Dr Philip Corder's paper on Romano-British Potters' Kilns[1] were issued as CBA Research Report No. 5. It gives an indication of the extent of, and gaps in, our present knowledge of these structures and is therefore useful as a guide to those interested in the excavation of kilns. A companion study of the range and dating of the products of the kilns, however, is still to be attempted.

Another important problem to be considered in studying a group of pottery is the extent to which the material is contemporary. When a site has been occupied over several centuries, the digging of pits and of deep foundation trenches is bound to have brought up sherds from earlier levels below, and these became distributed in levels later than their own. For the dating of any particular level it is possible that only a few sherds contemporary with its deposition will be crucial. Normally it is only these that need be studied and published, at least in areas where the general sequence of types and distribution of fabrics is already established. In other areas, however, it may sometimes be useful to publish larger quantities of sherds with the aim of showing the local range, even when not all are critical for dating, for pottery also shows the presence or absence of trade and cultural connections, and can sometimes throw light on matters of craftsmanship and taste.

Small modifications of design and even the introduction of new types cannot always be dated with precision. Ideally, exact dates are to be sought, but at present in practice it is often more convenient to refer to *periods*, with less clear-cut implications of exactitude. Particularly useful are the names of emperors and their dynasties in this connection, and the more important are listed below:

AD		*Periods to which common reference is made*
14–37	Tiberius	Tiberian ⎤
37–41	Caligula (Gaius)	⎟ pre-Flavian
41–54	Claudius	Claudian ⎟
54–68	Nero	Neronian ⎦
69–79	Vespasian ⎤	
79–81	Titus ⎬	Flavian
81–96	Domitian ⎦	
98–117	Trajan	Trajanic
117–138	Hadrian	Hadrianic
138–161	Pius ⎤	
161–180	Aurelius ⎬	Antonine
180–192	Commodus ⎦	
193–211	Severus ⎤	
211–217	Caracalla ⎟	
218–222	Elagabalus ⎬	Severan
222–235	Severus Alexander ⎦	
259–293	Various rulers	Gallic Empire
305–360	House of Constantine	Constantinian
379–395	Theodosius I	Theodosian

(NOTE: Combinations of these terms are also used, e.g. Hadrianic-Antonine and normally in the sense of late Hadrianic to early Antonine.)

[1] From *Archaeol J*, **104** for 1957 (1959), 10–27: the Research Report is now out of print.

Glossary of terms

The following list of terms and their definitions rests on a fair consensus of qualified opinion. Usage, even among experts, is not yet fully standardized.

Reference is given wherever possible to published examples, and considerable use is made of the two important basic studies by M R Hull (Hawkes and Hull, *Camulodunum*, Research Report of the Society of Antiquaries, London, No. 14, 1947) and J P Gillam (see p. 17). The use of Latin terms has been avoided unless there is no modern equivalent; self-evident terms are excluded.

It has been thought convenient to classify the terms into the following categories:
1. General terms.
2. Terms used of types of fabric or centres of manufacture.
3. Names given to particular classes of vessels sharing form and function.
4. Terms used for manufacturing techniques, decoration, and parts of vessels.

General terms

It is not possible to deal with all the general terms used in the study of pottery, but some common and useful ones are best defined here.

Association
Vessels are said to be in association with each other or with other objects if all are found together in one deposit.

Class
Vessels are said to belong to the same class if they are of the same general form and usable for the same purpose, irrespective of date, fabric, and details of form.

Group
Vessels are said to form a group if they are found in association in circumstances implying that they were made, used, discarded, or deposited at about the same point in time.

Rubbish survival
A vessel or sherd is described as a rubbish survival when there is evidence suggesting that it was broken or discarded significantly before the date of the deposit in which it is found. The terms *residual* or *stray* are sometimes used in this sense, too.

Survival
A vessel is called a survival when there is evidence suggesting that it was out of fashion when last used.

Type
Vessels are said to be of the same type if they are identical in all significant features of form and fabric and not merely similar in general appearance.

Type series
When vessels of the same class but of different types are arranged in chronological order and a trend of development is observed they are said to form a type-series.

Ware
A term used in two senses: vessels from the same production centres (e.g. New Forest ware), or vessels having the same basic characteristics in technique (e.g. colour-coated ware).

6

Terms used for manufacturing techniques, decoration, and parts of vessels

Appliqué
A term describing a figure or motive made separately and fixed to the surface of a vessel, *Antiq J*, **37** (1957), 39–42; for a mould, *Archaeol Aeliana*, 4th series, **11** (1962), pl. iv, fig. 1.

Barbotine (Fig. 2, No. 18)
A method of relief decoration produced by trailing semi-liquid clay on the vessel. Examples are ivy leaves on samian forms 35 and 36 and their imitations, and scrolls and figures on colour-coated beakers, some of which were produced in the Nene Valley and at Colchester, VCH. *Huntingdonshire*, 1, 1926, pls. iv vi, and *The Roman Potters' Kilns at Colchester*, 1963, Research Report of the Society of Antiquaries, London, No. 21, 91–9.

Bead rim
A rim in the form of a small, rounded moulding, in section at least two-thirds of a circle. It was often used on bowls, dishes and jars.

Biconical
A vessel is said to be biconical when the sides make a sharp, inward change of direction, as if two truncated cones were placed base to base. *Camulodunum*, form 241.

Burnished
A term used to describe a smooth, somewhat shiny surface produced by the application of a tool to the clay when it had reached leather-hard state.

Carination (Fig. 1, No. 7)
An angular inward change of direction of the wall of a vessel, often near the centre.

Cavetto rim
A rim, found especially on the black-burnished cooking pot, which curves outwards from the shoulder of the vessel to form a concave, quarter-round profile. The use of the term *cavetto rim jar* for the black-burnished cooking pot in general is imprecise.

Colour-coat
See slip and *colour-coated wares.*

Combing and comb stabbing
Decoration made with a comb, either drawn across the vessel to form linear, diagonal, or wavy patterns or used to make a series of stabbing marks.

Cordon (Fig. 3, No. 28)
A raised, continuous, horizontal band on the outer surface of a vessel.

Cornice rim
The rim of rough-cast and other beakers shaped like a delicate cornice moulding.

Corrugated (Fig. 3, No. 31)
A ripple effect in the wall of a vessel, resembling a series of grooves and cordons.

Countersunk handle
A rounded handle, partly sunk into the side of a vessel.

Cross-hatching
See lattice.

Disc rim, disc mouth
A flagon rim, the top of which is in the form of a disc.

Everted rim
A rim which turns sharply outwards from the shoulder of the vessel.

Fabric
A term used to describe the material of a finished vessel, including texture and colour of both paste and surface.

Flange
A prominent, continuous projection from the body or rim of a vessel. It may vary widely in form or position; it was intended to facilitate handling.

Flanged neck
A flagon neck which has a flange roughly halfway down the neck.

Foot-ring
A low pedestal-like ring formed on the base of a vessel to enable it to stand more securely.

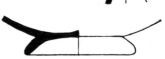

8

Frilling (Fig. 2, No. 27)

A decoration made with the fingers and similar to that put on the edge of a pie-crust. It is sometimes called *pie-crust decoration*, and is found on most tazze.

Fumed

A term which has been somewhat misleadingly used to describe the dark surface of vessels, in particular black-burnished ware, which has been exposed to a reducing atmosphere during the later stages of manufacture.

Furrowing

Decoration made by drawing the fingers or a tool across the body of a vessel, resulting in either a series of horizontal grooves or random groups of striations. *Verulamium, A Belgic and Two Roman Cities,* Society of Antiquaries Research Report No. 11 (1936), pls. xlix, No. 8 and li, No. 20, and *Richborough II*, pl. 29.

Girth Groove (Fig. 2, No. 15)

A continuous horizontal groove around the belly of a vessel.

Glaze

A vitreous or glassy layer fused on to the surface of a pot, as in St Rémy ware. This term is not correctly used to describe any other type of shiny surface.

Indented (Fig. 3, No. 32)

Used of the sides of a vessel which have been regularly pushed in to form a series of oval concavities; described also as *thumb-indented, dimpled,* and *folded.*

Kick

The raised centre of a base which rises to a hollow peak.

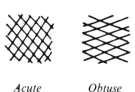

Lattice

Decoration formed by a criss-cross of diagonal lines, described as acute-angled if the angle to the horizontal is more than 45° and obtuse-angled if less than this; also known as *cross-hatching.*

Acute   *Obtuse*

Leather-hard

The state of a vessel after it has been air-dried, before firing.

Looped handles

Small sharply curving handles, fixed to the body of a vessel without being countersunk.

9

Mica-gilt (also known as **mica-dusted**)
The application of particles of mica to the surface of a vessel, giving it a golden sheen. Made in the 1st century at Gloucester. *Trans Bristol & Gloucester Archaeol Soc*, **91** (1972), 18–59.

Omphalos
A prominent hollow dome, raised in the base of a vessel.

Oxidized fabric
A fabric due to the firing of the vessel in the presence of oxygen, resulting usually in a light or red surface colouring.

Paint
A white or coloured slip applied as decoration, before firing, to the surface of a vessel with a brush or other implement.

Paste
The prepared clay from which pots are thrown. In the finished vessel the term is often applied to the body of a vessel, as distinct from the outer surface.

Pie-crust
See frilling.

Pinched neck
A type of flagon top pinched by finger and thumb into the form of a figure-of-eight to facilitate pouring.

Reduced fabric
A fabric produced when the final stages of heating and cooling are carried out in the absence of oxygen, resulting usually in a grey or black surface colouring.

Reeding (Fig. 2, No. 22)
The regular horizontal grooving on the flange of some types of mortaria and on the rim of some types of bowl.

Rilling
Fine close-set, horizontal lines formed by scribing with a tool on the body of a vessel, found, for example, on calcite-gritted jars.

Ring neck
The mouldings on a flagon neck in a series of super-imposed rings; also known less correctly as *screw neck*.

Roller-stamped

Decoration applied by a roller on which small panels of design have been cut, in three, four, or more patterns which are repeated on the vessel. Not to be confused with *stamped wares* which have no regular sequence of pattern but a haphazard arrangement due to the use of one or more independent dies (*see also Argonne ware*).

Rouletting(Fig. 1, No. 8)

Decoration made by a toothed or engraved wheel or a pliable sharp-edged tool, held against the vessel while it turns on the wheel.

Screw neck

A flagon neck with a continuous, spiral groove; not to be confused with *ring neck*.

Slip

Used both of (a) a fluid mixture of water and clay (with or without the addition of colouring agents) into which a vessel can be dipped, and of (b) the resulting coat after firing. (*See also colour-coated wares* and *paint*).

String marks

The marks on the bases of vessels caused by the potter detaching the pot from the wheel by means of a wire or string.

Wheel marks

The spiral marks, usually on the inside of a vessel, caused by the potter's fingers as the pot revolves on the wheel.

Terms used of types of fabric or centres of manufacture

Argonne ware

Pottery, usually with a red colour-coat, decorated with horizontal bands of impressed geometric patterns, executed with a roller stamp. The ware was made in the Argonne in north-east Gaul (G. Chenet, *La Céramique gallo-romaine d'Argonne du IVe siècle et la terre sigillée décorée à la molette,* 1941). It is sometimes called Marne ware; its distribution in Britain is mainly confined to the south and south-east and belongs to the 4th century. *Richborough I*, Research Report of the Society of Antiquaries of London No. 6 (1926), No. 95 and *Archaeol Cantiana*, **63** (1950), 96.

Black-burnished ware

The use of this term with a hyphen is proposed for distinctive forms of cooking pots, dishes, and bowls made from c. AD 120. The paste is usually granular and dense black. The surface of the bowls and dishes is completely and that of the cooking pots partly burnished. Cooking pots are decorated with latticing, with wavy or looped lines, or with arcs (Gillam, types 116–148, 218–228, 306–321). It has often been termed *fumed ware* or *cooking pot ware.* There are two distinguishable fabrics—Category 1, based on natives wares (*Proc Prehistoric Soc*, **24** (1958), 103), made in Dorset in surface kilns of the bonfire type, and 2, a greyer version with a silvery finish made at Rossington Bridge, near Doncaster. Other similar wares were made at Camulodunum and in Kent, and in the 3rd and 4th centuries there were many imitations, as at Lincoln (The Race Course Kiln, see below p. 23; for a general account of the problems of these wares see *CBA Research Report* No. 10 (1973), 63–103).

Calcite-gritted ware

Pottery in which particles of shell, limestone grit, calcite, etc., have been added to the clay; used especially for storage jars and cooking pots. Where the particles have been lost, leaving hollow spaces, the term *vesicular* has been used. A fabric made throughout the occupation but unevenly distributed and much more common in some areas in the 4th century than earlier.

Castor ware

This term has been loosely used for all kinds of colour-coated wares. It should be limited, if used at all, to those known to have been produced in the Castor area near Peterborough (but see, however, *Castor box*, p. 17): Artis, *The Durobrivae of Antoninus*, 1828; *VCH Northamptonshire*, 1 (1902), 206–13, and *VCH Huntingdonshire*, 1 (1926), 238–46; B R Hartley, *Notes on the Roman Pottery Industry in the Nene Valley* (1960), published by the Peterborough Museum; and *CBA Research Report* No. 10.

Colour-coated wares

Pottery which has been dipped into a slip rich in iron compounds; the colour of the slip varies but is usually darker than the paste, and occasionally the surface has a metallic lustre. These wares, although produced earlier, became very popular in the 3rd and 4th centuries. (*See also Argonne, Castor, New Forest, Oxfordshire, Rhenish, rough-cast,* and *varnished wares.*)

Crambeck ware

Pottery made at Crambeck, 4 miles south-east of Malton, Yorkshire, and widely distributed in the second half of the 4th century. Nearly half the products of these kilns consisted of straight-sided, flanged bowls and dishes, in lead-grey fabric, lightly burnished, and often having an internal wavy line. There are also buff and cream wares with red-painted decoration, and mortaria., P Corder, *The Roman Pottery at Crambeck, Castle Howard,* Roman Malton and District Report No. 1, 1928, and *Antiq J,* **17** (1937), 392–413.

Dales ware

A distinctive form of cooking pot common in northern England and the north-east Midlands in the 3rd and 4th centuries. The fabric is hard and coarse with a smooth but unpolished surface, grey, black, or brown in colour. The body of the clay contains small fragments of white shell. *Antiq J,* **31** (1951), 154–64.

Derbyshire ware

A distinctive ware produced in Derbyshire from the late 2nd century onwards. It is hard and gritty with a surface like 'petrified gooseflesh', the colour varying from grey and light-brown to red. The surface texture is due to the presence of silica particles in the local clay. All vessels are jars, mostly with a lid-seating on the rim. *Antiq J,* **19** (1939), 429–37; *Derbyshire Archaeol J,* **82** (1962), 21–42.

Eggshell ware (Fig. 1, No. 1)

Small beakers, bowls, or jars, usually in white or cream, but occasionally black ware, the sides of the vessels being 2 mm or even less in thickness. It was imported in the 1st century. (*Camulodunum,* forms 64 and 65) and imitated in Britain. Holt, *Y Cymmrodor,* **41** (1930), 163–4 and fig. 71, Nos. 171–74.

Gallo-Belgic ware

Vessels imported from Gaul in the 1st century, both before and after AD 43, in black or silver-grey fabric (*terra nigra*), or white fabric coated with red slip (*terra rubra*), or a dense white or cream fabric like pipeclay. Close British imitations of these fabrics and forms are known, and further copying of the forms was widespread (*Camulodunum,* p. 202). The imported vessels often have the name of the potter stamped on the inner surface of the base, a practice imitated in Britain but usually with illegible markings. V Rigby, *CBA Research Report* No. 10 (1973), 7–24.

Glevum ware
See Severn Valley ware

Holt ware
Pottery made at the legionary works-depot at Holt, Denbighshire, in the late 1st and early 2nd centuries (*Y Cymmrodor*, **41** (1930)) in light-red and buff fabric, often imitating samian forms, and found mostly in Chester and adjacent areas.

Huntcliff ware
A distinctive variety of calcite-gritted pottery limited to a range of distinctive forms. It was made in East Yorkshire throughout the occupation. The fabric is black or dark brown. The dishes and jar bodies were hand-made. A distinctive thick-walled cooking pot having a heavy curved rim, often with a groove on the inside of the lip, was extremely common throughout the north in the late 4th century. *J Roman Stud*, **2** (1912), 227; *Archaeol J*, **89** for 1932 (1933), 242–4.

Legionary wares
Distinctive types of pottery in use by the legions in Britain especially in the 1st century, when local products were found to be inadequate. These wares peculiar to each legion have been identified at Wroxeter, Lincoln, York, and Caerleon (*Archaeol Cambrensis*, **115** (1966), 45–66), but only at Chester is a production centre known at Holt where there was a works depot for tile-making.

London ware (Fig. 1, No. 2)
A term given to pottery often imitating samian forms 29, 30, and 36, in dark grey or black ware with a polished surface decorated with compass-scribed circles, incised groups of lines, and impressed stamps and rouletting (*Proc Suffolk Inst Archaeol*, **26** (1952), figs. 10, 11; *Antiq J*, **21** (1941), fig. 10). The distribution is widespread from several factories in southern Britain during the late 1st and 2nd centuries.

New Forest ware
Pottery made in the New Forest in the 3rd and 4th centuries, first studied by Heywood Sumner (*The New Forest Potteries*, 1927) and latterly by Vivian Swan (*CBA Research Report* No. 10 (1973), 117–34) and Michael Fulford (*The New Forest Roman Pottery*, BAR No. 17, 1975). The most distinctive type is the very hard, almost stoneware in a purple colour-coat with a metallic lustre in the form of indented beakers. There are other wares in grey and white in a wide range of vessels, some with a very local distribution (for a mid-4th century assemblage *see Portchester* I (1975), 282 ff.).

Oxfordshire wares

Pottery made mostly in the vicinity of Oxford in a variety of wares and vessels including distinctive types of mortaria, parchment wares, and red colour-coated ware in the samian tradition. This centrally placed industry became in the 4th century one of the largest and most important in Britain. *CBA Research Report*, No. 10 (1973), 105–15; for kilns *see Oxoniensia*, **38** (1973), 207–32; **39** (1975), 1–25.

Parisian ware

A thin, dark grey, highly burnished ware decorated with impressed stamps and found mainly in Yorkshire and Lincolnshire; of late 1st and 2nd century date. *Yorkshire Archaeol J*, **39** (1956), 48–52.

Patch Grove ware

Pottery in 'porridgy' grey paste with orange or brown surface, found mainly in north-west Kent or Surrey, usually in the form of wide-mouthed storage jars and with notched decoration on the shoulder. (*Archaeologia*, **90** (1944), 175 and fig. 9.) It is in a native tradition but lasted into the 2nd century.

Pevensey ware

A small local factory near Pevensey which produced imitations of Oxfordshire and New Forest types in a very hard orange-red paste and a deep red colour-coat. *Sussex Archaeol Collect*, **111** (1973), 41–4.

Rhenish ware

Pottery from Gaul and the Rhineland imported into Britain during the late 2nd century and later. It has a thin red paste and a black metallic colour coat, and some of the vessels are decorated with scrolls or sometimes words in in fine white paint (*see also motto-beaker*). The commonest form is an indented rouletted beaker (Gillam, types 44–46). Close imitations appear to have been made in the Nene Valley.

Romano-Saxon ware

This term is used both of wheel-made Roman pottery in coarse or colour-coated fabrics with stamped or bossed decoration resembling that on many hand-made Saxon vessels, and also of hand-made Saxon pottery imitating Roman forms. It is found mainly in eastern England. (*The Anglo-Saxon Cemeteries of Caistor-by-Norwich and Markshall, Norfolk* (1973), 31–2). The former class belongs to the late 3rd and 4th centuries and is not to be confused with such stamped wares of earlier periods as *London* and *Parisian wares*. J N L Myres in *Dark-Age Britain* (1956), 16–39; *Anglo-Saxon Pottery and the Settlement of England* (1969).

Rough-cast ware (Fig. 1, No. 3)

Pottery, often coloured or varnished, having particles of dried clay or similar material dusted over the surface; also (probably incorrectly) called *sand-faced*.

Rustic ware (Fig. 1, No. 4)

Pottery, mainly jars, usually in grey fabric with knobs or ridges of clay either applied or drawn from the surface of the vessel. It belongs to the 1st and 2nd centuries, but some was made in the 3rd century in East Anglia. *Antiq J*, **38** (1958), 15–51.

St Rémy ware

Fine pottery, often with relief decoration, in a white fabric with a green or yellow (lead) glaze, made at St Rémy-en-Rollat, near Vichy. Small jars, bowls, and flagons were imported into Britain in the 1st century. *The Roman Pottery found at Silchester*, 1916, pl. xl, published by Reading Museum, and *The Roman Town and Villa at Great Casterton, Rutland*, 1951, fig. 5, No. 1, published by the University of Nottingham. Imitations were made in Britain up to the mid-2nd century, as at Little Chester, Derby (*Antiq J*, **51** (1971), 36–9).

Severn Valley ware

Burnished wares mainly in the form of bowls, jars, and tankards in a colour range from creamy-buff to orange-red made at various centres along the Severn. Kiln sites are known at Malvern, Perry Barr, Birmingham (*Trans Birmingham Archaeol Soc*, **77** (1961), 33–9) and Shepton Mallet, Somerset. It was at one time known as *Glevum ware*, since it was first recognized at Gloucester (*J Roman Stud*, **33** (1943), 15–28; for ware produced in Gloucester *see Trans Bristol and Gloucs Archaeol Soc*, **91** (1972), 18–59. It is found all over the Severn Valley and small quantities reached the western part of Hadrian's Wall (*Archaeol Aeliana*, **50** (1972), 191–203).

Terra Nigra, Terra Rubra

See Gallo-Belgic wares.

Upchurch ware

A term once used widely of types of polished or burnished black and grey wares (e.g. poppy-head beakers), thought to have been made in the Upchurch Marshes, Kent. There were undoubtedly kilns in this area, but until a thorough study has been made of their products, the use of this term is better avoided. T Wright, *Wanderings of an Antiquary* (1854), 162–71.

Varnished ware

Pottery, usually small bowls, decorated with rough-cast scales or roundels, or rough-cast beakers in white fabric with greenish-brown shiny slip; of 1st century date and produced in central Gaul and on the Rhine. *CBA Research Report* No. 10 (1973), 25–37.

Vesicular ware

See Calcite-gritted ware.

Names given to particular classes of vessels sharing form and function

Amphora (Fig. 3, Nos. 33–35)

A large, two-handled container, varying in shape and fabric, but with a rounded or pointed base, used for importing oil, wine, etc. (for forms *see London in Roman Times* (1930), pls. liv and lv, published by The London Museum.) Sometimes there are stamps on the handles, more rarely on the neck, body, or base, denoting the name of the maker of the vessel or the producer of the contents, or both. M H Callender, *Roman Amphorae* (1965). The rim or body may be painted or scratched with letters or numerals denoting ownership, capacity, contents, or vintage.

Beaker (Fig. 1, No. 5)

A drinking vessel of suitable size and shape to hold in the hands. The precise type is normally specified by reference to form or fabric; e.g. butt-beaker, rough-cast beaker.

Bowl (Fig. 1, No. 2)

A neckless vessel, which can be conveniently defined as having a height more than one-third of but not greater than its diameter.

Butt-beaker (Fig. 1, No. 6)

A tall beaker shaped like a butt or barrel and having a small, everted rim; the vessel is usually decorated with cordons, rouletting, latticing, etc., and normally of mid-1st century date. Some were Gallo-Belgic and others locally made. *Camulodunum*, forms 112–116.

Campanulate bowl

A bowl in the form of an inverted bell, as in samian form 27.

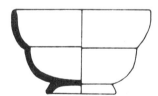

Carinated bowl (Fig. 1, No. 7)

A term often applied to a specific type of bowl or jar with a flat or reeded rim and an almost vertical upper wall above a sharp inward change of direction. Gillam, types 214–218.

Castor box (Fig. 1, No. 8)

A shallow vessel in colour-coated ware with a fitting lid. Usually both box and lid were rouletted. Gillam, types 341 and 342.

Cheese press or wring (Fig. 1, No. 9)

A small, shallow, flat-bottomed dish with holes and concentric ridges in the bottom; presumed to have been manufactured for cheese-making. Correspondingly ridged lids without holes are known. *Camulodunum*, form 199, and Gillam, type 350.

Cooking pot

A term usually used for jars which are known from soot-incrustation to have been used for cooking. In the North of Britain, however, the term, when used without qualification, is restricted to cooking pots in black-burnished fabric whose thin hand-finished walls do not have internal wheel-marks, e.g. Gillam, type 125.

Costrel (Fig. 1, No. 10)

A rare type of vessel shaped like a barrel on its side with small neck and handles on the top and small stud-like feet on the bottom. The body is often rilled to imitate a barrel. Gillam, type 21.

Dish (Fig. 1, No. 11)

A shallow vessel, which can be conveniently defined as having a height less than one-third of but greater than one-seventh of its diameter (*see also pie-dish*).

Face Urn (Fig. 1, No. 12)

A jar with a human face, usually in appliqué technique, formed on the shoulder. The function of these vessels was often funerary (*Roman Colchester*, Research Report of the Society of Antiquaries, London, No. 20, 1958, types 288–290). There are also flagons with faces moulded on the neck (*Richborough II*, Research Report of the Society of Antiquaries of London, No. 7, 1928, No. 184).

Flagon (Fig. 1, Nos. 13 and 14)

A vessel used for holding liquids, with a narrow neck, usually a globular body, a foot-ring, and one or more handles (*see also jug, lagena*, and *Hofheim flagon*).

Flower vase

See Triple vase

Girth beaker (Fig. 2, No. 15)

A vertical-sided beaker, with horizontal bands of corrugations, cordons, latticing, etc. of mid-1st century date. Some were Gallo-Belgic and others locally made. *Camulodunum*, forms 82–94. See also *Butt-beaker*.

Hofheim flagon (Fig. 2, No. 16)

Single- and doubled-handled flagons with cylindrical necks and out-curved lips, triangular in section, of the 1st century; named from the mid-1st century site at Hofheim. *Camulodunum*, forms 140 and 161.

Honey jar (Fig. 2, No. 17)

A double-handled jar with wide mouth. *Camulodunum*, form 175.

Hunt cup (Fig. 2, No. 18)

A type of colour-coated beaker decorated with animals in barbotine, usually hounds hunting deer or hares.

Incense cup

See Tazza

Jar (Fig. 2, No. 19)

A vessel with a constriction at the neck whose width is usually less than its height. It is convenient also to distinguish wide-mouthed, medium-mouthed, and narrow-mouthed jars. This term in general excludes flagons and beakers *(see also cooking pot, face urn* and *honey jar)*.

Jug (Fig. 2, No. 20)

A flagon or handled jar with a spout.

Lagena

A term sometimes used for a large, two-handled flagon, at least 0·5 m high, to be distinguished from amphora. J Curle, *A Roman Frontier Post and its People, the Fort at Newstead*, 1911, Glasgow, pl. xlix (B), fig. 1, and p. 267.

Mortarium (plural *mortaria)* (Fig. 2, No. 21)

A bowl-shaped vessel with a rim adapted for gripping and a spout. Grit is usually embedded in its inner surface, which is of segmental section. Rims vary greatly in form *(Wroxeter I,* Research Report of the Society of Antiquaries of London, No. 1, 1913, 76–89) and are distinguished by such special terms as *hammer-headed* (No. 22) and *wall-sided* (No. 23). They were used primarily for mixing food. First- and second-century examples often have the name of the maker stamped on each or one side of the spout, or the name on one side and FECIT on the other. *Archaeol Aeliana*, 4th series, **26** (1948), 172–204; *CBA Research Report* No. 10 (1974), 39–51.

Motto beaker

A beaker made in Gaul and the Rhineland decorated with white-painted scrolls and words forming phrases such as DA MIHI VINVM (Give me wine), VALETE and VIVAS (Good health), NOLITE SITIRE (Thirst not), BIBE (Drink up), etc. M Bös, Aufschriften auf rheinischen Trinkgefässen der Römerzeit, *Kölner Jahrbuch für Vor- und Frühgeschichte* 3 (1958).

Mug

See Tankard

Olla

An obsolete term, formerly used for cooking pots and jars.

Pedestal-beaker (Fig. 2, No. 24)

A beaker with a pedestal foot; some are Gallo-Belgic, others locally made. *Camulodunum* forms 71–81.

Pie-dish (Fig. 1, No. 11)

A term sometimes used for a dish with a flat rim, usually in black-burnished ware and often decorated with a lattice pattern on the side and loops on the outside of the base. There is no evidence that it was used as the name suggests.

Plate, Platter

A shallow vessel, in height not greater than one-seventh of its diameter.

Poppy-head beaker (Fig. 3, No. 28)
A beaker shaped like the seed-head of a poppy in grey or black fabric with a polished surface. It has an everted rim and the body is often decorated with panels of barbotine dots or rouletting. The largest sizes could be classified as jars.

Segmental bowl
A term sometimes used for a hemispherical bowl (as in Fig. 1, No. 2), the body forming part of the segment of a sphere.

Spouted strainer
A type of bowl, usually biconical, having a projecting tubular spout with an internal strainer, probably used for wine.

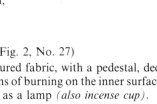

Storage jar
A large jar used for storing grain or other materials.

Tankard, Mug (Fig. 2, No. 26)
A single-handled drinking vessel (Gillam, types 64–66, 179–183).

Tazza (pronounced *tatsa*; plural *tazze*: Fig. 2, No. 27)
A cup-like vessel, usually in a light-coloured fabric, with a pedestal, decorated with bands of frilling. There are often signs of burning on the inner surface and it was probably used in religious ritual or as a lamp *(also incense cup)*.

Triple vase (Fig. 2, No. 25)
A vessel usually with three small jars, either attached to the top of a tubular ring-base which is often hollow, or joined together at the body. Such vessels have also been described as *flower vases*. W J Kaye, *Roman and other Triple Vases*, 1914, London, Elliot Stock.

Tripod bowl (Fig. 3, No. 29)
A bowl with three legs, normally of 1st century date. *Camulodunum*, form 45.

Unguent flask (Fig. 3, No. 30)
A small narrow-necked vessel, usually in a rough fabric, sometimes reeded; thought to have been a container for ointment or perfume, and imported.

A list of stratified groups

A large amount of pottery has already been published but much of it is not well stratified or in contemporary groups. There are some publications, however, which illustrate numbers of complete vessels and these should provide a useful guide in assessing the shape and size of particular vessels represented by small pieces. These publications include:

T May, *The Pottery found at Silchester* (1916) published by the Reading Museum. This is the only publication of the pottery from the extensive series of excavations carried out on the Roman town by the Society of Antiquaries from 1890 to 1909.

T May, *Catalogue of the Roman Pottery in the Colchester and Essex Museum* (1930), CUP.

W Whiting, N Hawley, and T May, *Excavations of the Roman Cemetery at Ospringe, Kent* (1931).

J P Bushe-Fox, *The Excavation of the Roman Fort at Richborough, Kent*, I (1926); II (1928); 111 (1932); IV (1949); V (1968). In these five reports there are 623 vessels illustrated, almost all of them with complete sections. The find spots are given and dating evidence can be established for most of the pottery.

M R Hull, *Roman Colchester* (1958) extends the *Camulodunum* series with useful comments on dates.

Malcolm Todd, The commoner late Roman coarse wares of the East Midlands, *Antiq J*, **48** (1968), 192–209.

Eburacum, Roman York, RCHM (1962) includes a useful series of vessels from cemeteries.

The following are some of the publications of well dated groups and vessels of prime importance to the student:

J P Gillam, Types of Roman Coarse Pottery Vessels in Northern Britain, *Arch Ael*, 4th series, **35** (1957), 180–251. Republished with additional notes as a third edition in 1970 by The Oriel Press Ltd, 27 Ridley Place, Newcastle upon Tyne 1. [This should now be used with the reconsidered dating of the Corbridge destruction deposit by B R Hartley, *Britannia*, **3** (1972), 45–8]

C F C Hawkes and M R Hull, *Camulodunum* (1947) illustrates a very fine series of 1st century types of imported and native wares.

Sheppard Frere, *Verulamium Excavations*, I (1972) includes a fine dated series catalogued by Marion Wilson, 265–372.

Barry Cunliffe, *Excavations at Portchester Castle*, (I (1975) includes a well organized pottery section by Michael Fulford but almost entirely of 4th century wares, 270–366.

An attempt has been made below to present a selection of stratified groups which may be helpful to the student. The list has been arranged on a regional basis and covers only Britain south of the northern frontier, for which area J P Gillam has already published his type series. It has to be admitted that the list as an uneven quality: good groups for some areas are excluded and poor ones from others included. The reason for this is that the amount of published material varies very much from one county to another and an attempt has to be made to cover the whole country. It is hoped that the list will soon be outdated with the publication of new and better groups filling some of the gaps. In a few cases, amended dating is suggested; these minor adjustments are offered in the light of improved knowledge, with due apology to the excavators concerned.

The Northern Frontier Zone [See J. P. Gillam's type series]

Yorkshire

Roman Malton: The Civilian Settlement, by N Mitchelson, *Yorkshire Archaeol J*, **41** (1966), 209–61, includes small groups groups from the late 1st to the late 4th century.

Belgic and other early pottery found at N. Ferriby, Yorks., by Philip Corder and T Davies Pryce, *Antiq J*, **18** (1938), 262–77. Mid-1st century.

Excavations at Brough-on-Humber 1958–61, by J S Wacher, 1969, Soc of Antiq Research Report No. 25, includes some good Antonine and later groups.

The Roman Fort at Bainbridge, Excavations of 1957–9, by B R Hartley, *Proc Leeds Phil Lit Soc*, **9** (1960). 107–31. Small groups of all periods from *c*. AD 80.

A Roman Pottery Kiln in the Parish of Lockington by G D Lloyd, *East Riding Archaeologist*, **1.1** (1968), 27–38, *c*. AD 150–250.

The Defences of Isurium Brigantum (Aldborough), by J N L Myres, K A Steer, and Mrs A M H Chitty, *Yorkshire Archaeol J*, **40** (1959), 1–77. Small groups from the 2nd to the 4th centuries.

The Roman Pottery at Norton, East Yorkshire, by R H Hayes and Sir Edward Whitley, 1950 (Roman Malton and District Report No. 7). 3rd century.

Cataractonium. Fort and Town, by E J W Hildyard, *Yorkshire Archaeol J*, **39** (1957), 224–65. Pottery report by J P Gillam includes an important late 4th century group, figs. 10–14.

The Roman Pottery at Crambeck, Castle Howard, by Philip Corder, 1928 (Roman Malton and District Report No. 1), with modified dating in A Pair of Fourth-Century Romano-British Pottery Kilns near Crambeck, by Philip Corder and Margaret Birley, *Antiq J*, **17** (1937), 392–413. Mainly late 4th century.

The Pottery from the Roman Signal-Stations on the Yorkshire Coast, by M R Hull, *Archaeol J*, **89** for 1932 (1933), 220–53. Late 4th century.

The North-West: Cheshire, Lancashire, and N. Staffordshire

Cheshire

Excavations at Heronbridge, 1947–8, by B R Hartley. *J Chester N Wales Architect Archaeol Hist Soc*, **39** (1952), 1–20. Late 1st to early 2nd century groups (A–C, figs. 9 and 10) a group *c*. AD 120–180 (E, figs. 10 and 11).

Lancashire

Excavations on the site of the Roman Fort at Lancaster, 1950, by I A Richmond, *Trans Hist Soc Lancashire Cheshire*, **105** (1953), 1–23. The pottery report by J P Gillam includes 3rd century groups.

Manchester

Roman Manchester (1974) by G D B Jones includes a pottery report by Peter Webster with a good Flavian-Trajanic group, 89–118.

The East and North Midlands: Derbyshire, Leicestershire, Lincolnshire, Nottinghamshire, and Rutland

Derbyshire

An Excavation on the Roman Site at Little Chester, Derby, by Graham Webster, *Derbyshire Archaeol J*, **81** (1961), 85–110. An Antonine group.

A Trajanic kiln complex near Little Chester, Derby, 1968, by M Brassington, *Antiq J*, **51** (1971), 36–69. The dating may be a little too early.

Lincolnshire

A Romano-British Pottery Kiln at North Hykeham, Lincs., by F H Thompson, *Antiq J*, **38** (1958), 15–51. A late 1st century group including rustic ware, on the typology, dating, and distribution of which there is an Appendix.

A Roman Pottery at South Carlton, Lincs., by Graham Webster, *Antiq J*, **24** (1944), 129–43. A group of kiln-products of the late 2nd century, dated here too early.

A Romano-British Pottery Kiln on the Lincoln Racecourse, by Philip Corder (1950), University of Nottingham. A group of black-burnished wares of the early 3rd century.

The Excavation of a Romano-British Pottery Kiln at Swanpool, Lincoln, by Graham Webster and N Booth, *Antiq J*, **27** (1947), 61–79. An early to mid-4th century group, dated too early in the report.

Nottinghamshire

The Pottery of a Claudian Well at Margidunum, by F Oswald, *J Roman Stud*, **13** (1923), 114–26. The date of this deposit can probably be extended to *c*. AD 75.

The Pottery of a Third-Century Well at Margidunum, by F Oswald, *J Roman Stud*, **16** (1926), 36–44. Although dated by late 3rd century coins, there are probably early 4th century vessels as well as rubbish survivals.

Rutland

The Roman Town and Villa at Great Casterton, Rutland, University of Nottingham (1951), 24–40. Villa destruction deposit, last quarter of the 4th century, by J P Gillam. The Third Report under the same title for the years 1954–58, 1961, includes pre-Flavian and Flavian groups (fig. 14 and 15) and small groups of later periods. *The Roman Fort* (1968), 42–51, mid-1st century pottery.

East Anglia: Cambridgeshire, Huntingdonshire, Norfolk, and Suffolk

Cambridgeshire

The Roman Pottery from Coldham Clamp and its Affinities, by Timothy Potter, *Proc Cambridge Antiq Soc*, **58** (1965), 12–37, mainly 2nd century groups.

A Romano-British Settlement at Arbury Road, Cambridge, by W H C Frend, *Proc Cambridge Antiq Soc*, **48** for 1954 (1955), 10–43. The pottery report by B R Hartley includes five groups from pits, two of the 2nd century and three of the 4th century.

The Roman fortress at Longthorpe, by S S Frere and J K St Joseph, *Britannia*, **5** (1974), includes a group of mid-1st century wares, 96–109.

Norfolk

Roman Pottery from Caistor-next-Norwich, by D Atkinson, *Norfolk Archaeol*, **26** (1937), 197–230, includes groups from pits and stratified deposits, some dated by coins, but containing many rubbish survivals.

A Claudian Site at Needham, Norfolk, by Sheppard Frere, *Antiq J*, **21** (1941), 40–55. A small group of Claudian pottery.

The Romano-British Village at Needham, Norfolk, by Sheppard Frere and Rainbird Clarke. *Norfolk Archaeol*, **28** (1943), 187–216, includes 1st and 2nd century groups from pits.

Three Caistor Pottery Kilns, by D Atkinson, *J Roman Stud*, **22** (1932), 33–46. Early 2nd century groups.

Suffolk

Romano-British Pottery Kilns at West Stow Heath, by S E West, *Proc Suffolk Inst Archaeol*, **26.1** (1952), 35–53. Early 2nd century.

Some Suffolk Kilns: Two Kilns making Colour-coated Ware at Grimstone End, Pakenham, by N Smedley and E Owles, *Proc Suffolk Inst Archaeol*, **28.3** (1961), 203–25. 3rd century. *See also* A Romano-British Pottery Kiln at Homersfield, **28.2** (1959), 168–84, *c*. AD 300, and A Small Kiln at Grimstone End, Pakenham, **29.1** (1962), 67–72, early 2nd century.

The West Midlands: Herefordshire, Shropshire, S. Staffordshire, Warwickshire, and Worcestershire

Herefordshire

Excavations at Sutton Walls, Herefordshire, 1948–1951, by Kathleen M Kenyon, *Archaeol J*, **110** for 1953 (1954), 1–87. A late 2nd century group from a pit (figs. 15–17).

Shropshire

Excavations at Wroxeter, Shropshire, by J P Bushe-Fox, Soc of Antiq Research Reports Nos. 1, 2 and 4 (1912–4). Although not all securely stratified, contains some useful material, including a study of mortarium rims (1912).

Report on Excavations at Wroxeter, 1923–27, by Donald Atkinson (1942). A group pre-AD 130, figs. 42–44.

A Roman Pottery Factory near Wroxeter, by A W J Houghton, *Trans Shropshire Archaeol Soc*, **58** for 1962–63 (1964), 101–11, a 4th century group.

S Staffordshire

Excavations at Wall (Staffs) 1964–66, by J Gould, *Trans Lichfield S Staffs Archaeol Hist Soc*, **8** for 1966–67 (1968), 1–38, includes a Neronian group, figs. 12 and 13; **5** for 1963–64 (1964), includes an Antonine group, figs. 16 and 17.

Warwickshire

The Romano-British Potters' Field at Wappenbury, Warwickshire, by Muriel and Brian Stanley, *Trans Proc Birmingham Archaeol Soc*, **79** for 1960 and 61 (1964), 93–108. Kiln groups of the early 4th century.

Worcestershire

Romano-British pottery production in the Malvern District of Worcestershire, by D P S Peacock, *Trans Worcestershire Archaeol Soc*, **1**, 3rd ser. for 1965–67 (1968), 15–28.

Report on Excavations in Bays Meadow, Droitwich, by P S Gelling, *Trans Proc Birmingham Archaeol Soc*, **75** for 1957 (1959), 1–23. Includes a 4th century group from a pit (fig. 5).

Excavations on a Romano-British Site at Astley, 1956–58, by Ian Walker, *Trans Worcestershire Archaeol Soc*, **35** for 1958 (1959), 29–57, 2nd and 3rd century.

The South Midlands

Berkshire

Cox Green Roman Villa, by C M Bennett, *Berkshire Archaeol J*, **60** (1962), 62–91, some 4th century groups.

Buckinghamshire

The Excavation of a Romano-British Pottery Kiln Site, near Hedgerley, by K P Oakley, C E Vulliamy, E Clive Rouse, and Frank Cottrill, *Rec Buckinghamshire*, **13**.4 (1938), 252–80. A mid-2nd century group.

Northamptonshire

Excavations at Irchester, 1962–63, by D N Hall and N Nickerson, *Archaeol J*, **124** for 1967 (1968), 65–129. A group datable to *c*. AD 45–75, classified here as 'late-Belgic', figs. 10–13.

A Romano-British Pottery Kiln at Weston Favell, near Northampton, by Brian Bunch and Philip Corder, *Antiq J*, **34** (1954), 218–24. A small 1st century group.

Oxfordshire

On the Pottery from the Waste Heap of the Roman Potters' Kilns Discovered at Sandford, near Littlemore, Oxon. in 1879, by T May, *Archaeologia*, **72** (1922), 225–42. Now considered to be mainly 4th century.

Two Romano-British Potters' Fields near Oxford, by D B Harden, *Oxoniensia*, **1** (1936), 81–102. Two small 4th century groups.

A Romano-British Potters' Field at Cowley, Oxon., by R J C Atkinson, *Oxoniensia*, **6** (1941), 9–21. Mainly 4th century.

Excavations at Dorchester on Thames, 1962, by Sheppard Frere, *Archaeol J*, **119** for 1962 (1964), 114–49, includes a mid-1st century (fig. 12), small 2nd century (figs. 15, 16 and 17), and a 4th century group (fig. 18).

The 'Overdale' kiln site at Boar's Hill, near Oxford, by Eve Harris and Christopher J Young, *Oxoniensia*, **39** (1975), 12–25. A late 2nd century group.

London and the Home Counties: Essex, Hertfordshire, Kent, Middlesex and Surrey

Essex

The Roman Pottery Kilns of Colchester, by M R Hull, Soc of Antiq Research Report No. 21 (1963). Contains important kiln groups, including samian and colour-coated wares. *Roman Colchester*, by M R Hull, Soc of Antiq Research Report No. 20 (1958). Contains an important 4th century group from the Mithraeum but with rubbish survivals (figs. 60–71); a late 1st to early 2nd century group dated by decorated samian and a coin of Domitian, AD 77–78, in good condition (Insula 7, Pit 1, figs. 53–56).

Hertfordshire

Verulamium Excavations, I (1972) by Sheppard Frere contains a full stratified series.

A Roman Pottery of the Hadrian-Antonine period at Verulamium, by Philip Corder, *Antiq J*, **21** (1941), 271–98. A group from a pit dated by coins to AD 120–160.

Excavations on Verulam Hills Field, St Albans, 1963–64, by Ilid E Antony, *Hertfordshire Archaeol*, **1** (1968), 26–33, four small kiln groups c. AD 130–165.

The Roman Theatre at Verulamium, St Albans, by Kathleen M Kenyon, *Archaeologia*, **84** (1935), 213–61, fig. 11. A late 4th century group.

The Excavations of the Roman Villa in Gadebridge Park, Hemel Hempstead, 1963–68, by David S Neal, Soc of Antiq Research Report No. 31 (1974) contains a large mixed group from Ditch 1, mainly late 1st century but with some mid-2nd century pieces (Nos. 1–143, a mid-4th century group from Room 20 (Nos. 258–323), and some smaller groups.

Excavations in Colchester 1964–8, by B R K Dunnett, *Trans Essex Archaeol Soc*, **3** (1971), includes groups from the destruction of AD 60 (figs. 8 and 9).

The Roman Villa at Lockleys, Welwyn, by J B Ward Perkins, *Antiq J*, **18** (1938), 339–76, includes 4th century groups (figs. 9–11).

The Roman Villa at Park Street, near St Albans, Herts., by Helen O'Neil, *Archaeol J*, **102** for 1945 (1947), 21–110. Pottery report by Philip Corder includes 4th century groups (figs. 18 and 19).

Kent

Canterbury excavations include: Excavations in Burgate Street, 1956–8, by F Jenkins, *Archaeol Cantiana*, **63** (1950), 82–118 and Rose Lane, by S S Frere, *Archaeol Cantiana*, **68** (1954), 102–43, various small groups from pits and hearths; A Tilery and Pottery Kilns at Durovernum, by F Jenkins, *Antiq J*, **36** (1956), 40–56, fig. 8, a small mid-1st century group.

A First Century Urn-field at Cheriton, near Folkestone, by P J Tester and H F Bing, *Archaeol Cantiana*, **63** (1949), 21–36, vessels of the 1st and early 2nd century.

Lullingstone Villa Reports by G W Meates include a late 2nd to early 3rd century group from a well with rubbish survivals, *Archaeol Cantiana*, **66** (1953), 15–36; a 4th century group, *Archaeol Cantiana*, **63** (1950), 1–49, and a 4th century group, *Archaeol Cantiana*, **65** (1952), 26–78, Group iv, figs. 7 and 8.

Middlesex

Report on the Excavations at Brockley Hill, by K M Richardson, *Trans London Middlesex Archaeol Soc*, **10.1** (1948), 1–23. A group *c*. AD 80–120.

Excavations at Brockley Hill, by P G Suggett, *Trans London Middlesex Archaeol Soc*, **11.3** (1954), 259–76. A series of stamped mortaria and other wares, late 1st and early 2nd century and later.

Surrey

The Fourth Century Romano-British Kilns at Overwey, Tilford, by Antony J Clark, *Surrey Archaeol Collect*, **51** for 1948–9 (1950), 29–56; Romano-British Cemeteries at Haslemere and Charterhouse, by John Holmes, *Ibid*, 1–28. Include 1st and early 2nd century vessels.

Excavations at Southwark, by Kathleen M Kenyon, Surrey Archaeol Research Paper No. 5 (1959). Includes type series and stratified groups of mid-2nd century (fig. 21); late 2nd century (figs. 22 and 23), and 4th century (fig. 24), but includes rubbish survivals.

Excavations at Topping's and Sun Wharves, Southwark, 1970–72, by Harvey Sheldon, *Trans London Middlesex Archaeol Soc*, **25** (1974) contains late 1st century groups, 41–63.

Excavations at Aldgate and Bush Lane House 1972, by Hugh Chapman and Tony Johnson, *Trans London Middlesex Archaeol Soc*, **24** (1973) contains stratified 1st century groups, 18–39.

The Excavation of a Late Roman Bath-House at Chatley Farm, Cobham, by Sheppard Frere, *Surrey Archaeol Collect*, **50** for 1946–7 (1949), 73–98. A group of 4th century pottery (figs. 5–8).

The South: Dorset, Hampshire, Sussex, and Wiltshire

Dorset

Romano-British Settlement at Studland, Dorset, by N H Field, *Proc Dorset Natur Hist Archaeol Soc*, **87** for 1965 (1966), 142–99, small groups of the 1st, 3rd, and 4th centuries.

An Early Romano-British Kiln at Corfe Mullen, Dorset, by J B Calkin, *Antiq J*, **15** (1935), 42–55, a small mid-1st century group.

Hampshire

Winchester Excavations 1949–60, 1, City of Winchester Mus. and Libraries Committee (1964), by Barry Cunliffe, contains a number of small groups of various periods.

Report on the Excavations on the Roman Pottery Kiln at Hallcourt Wood, Shedfield, Hampshire, 1960, by Barry Cunliffe, *Proc Hampshire Fld Club Archaeol Soc*, **21.4** (1961), 8–24. 1st century.

Excavations at Silchester, 1938–9, by M Aylwin Cotton, *Archaeologia*, **92** (1947), 121–67. Includes 1st and 2nd century groups (Figs. 11, 12, and 16).

A Group of Pottery from Clausentum, by D Waterman, *Proc Hampshire Fld Club Archaeol Soc*, **17.3** (1952), 253–63. A Flavian group, dated too early in the report.

Excavations at Clausentum, 1937–8, by D M Waterman, *Antiq J.* **27** (1947), 151–71, includes 4th century pottery.

New Forest Roman Pottery by M G Fulford, BAR (1975) gives a detailed account of the manufacture and distribution and a corpus of types.

Sussex

The Roman Villa at Angmering, by Leslie Scott, *Sussex Archaeol Collect*, **79** (1938), 1–44, includes a late 1st to 2nd century group from the bath-house.

Excavation at a Site in North Street, Chichester, 1958–9, by K M E Murray and Barry Cunliffe, *Sussex Archaeol Collect*, **100** (1962), 93–110, includes 1st and 2nd century groups.

The Roman Cemetery at Chichester by G M Clark, *Sussex Archaeol Collect*, **80** (1939), 170–92, republished and expanded to 322 vessels in *Chichester Excavations*, I (1971), 89–122. Burial groups of the 2nd to the 4th century.

A Prehistoric and Romano-British Site at West Blatchington, Hove, by N E S Norris and G P Burstow, *Sussex Archaeol Collect*, **90** for 1951–2 (1952), 221–240. 4th century groups.

Excavations at Fishbourne, II, by Barry Cunliffe, Soc of Antiq Research Report No. 27 (1971) contains an account of the pottery, arranged as a type-series.

Wiltshire

A late first-century well at Cunetio, by F K Annable, *Wiltshire Archaeol Natur Hist Mag*, **61** (1966), 9–24.

A Romano-British Pottery in Savernake Forest: Kilns 1–2, by F K Annable, *Wiltshire Archaeol Natur Hist Mag*, **58** (1962), 142–55. Late 1st century.

Oare reconsidered and the origins of Savernake ware in Wiltshire, by V G Swan, *Britannia*, **6** (1975), 36–61.

The South-West: Cornwall, Devon, Gloucestershire, and Somerset

Cornwall

An Excavation at St Mawgan-in-Pyder, N Cornwall, by L Murray-Threipland, *Archaeol J*, **113** for 1956 (1957), 53–69, contains 1st century pottery with strong native influence, and also later pieces (figs. 18–32).

Devon

Roman Discoveries in Exeter, 1951–2, by Aileen Fox, *Proc Devon Archaeol Exploration Soc*, **4** (1951), 106–13. A small Flavian group (figs. 1 and 2) from a pit in Fore Street.

Roman Exeter, by Aileen Fox, Manchester University Press (1952), includes a 1st century group from South Street (fig. 14, Nos. 1–21; fig. 16, Nos. 23–29; fig. 17, Nos. 30–38) and a 3rd century group (figs. 17 and 18, Nos. 40–57, with rubbish survivals).

Gloucestershire

Report on the Excavations of the Prehistoric, Roman and Post-Roman Site in Lydney Park, Glos., by R E M and T V Wheeler, Soc of Antiq Research Report No. 9 (1932), includes late 4th century groups (figs. 26 and 27).

Roman pottery kilns at Gloucester, by Bernard Rawes, *Trans Bristol & Glouces Archaeol Soc*, **91** (1972), 18–59, with a period of production *c*. AD 70–110.

Excavations at the new Market Hall, Gloucester, 1966–7, by Mark Hassall and John Rhodes, *Trans Bristol & Glouces Archaeol Soc*, **93** (1975), contains a large quantity of pottery analysed in a type series, only a small amount stratified, 41–66.

Somerset

The Roman Site at Catsgore, Somerton, by C A Ralegh Radford, *Proc Somerset Archaeol Natur Hist Soc*, **96** (1952), 41–77. A small Antonine group, dated too early in the report (fig. 7, Nos. 1–10).

The Temple Well at Pagans Hill, Chew Stoke, by P Rahtz and L G Harris, *Proc Somerset Archaeol Natur Hist Soc*, 101–2 for 1956–7 (1958), 15–51. A small group of the late 3rd century for a well, dated by a coin of Postumus (fig. 4, Nos. 1–16).

The West

Wales and Monmouthshire

Caerleon: Jenkins's Field, 1926, by V E Nash-Williams, *Archaeol Cambrensis*, **84** (1929), 280–353. Includes a Flavian group from a pit dated by a coin of Vespasian (AD 77–78) and samian (Nos. 2–5, 7–9, 12, 18–20, 41, 44, 58, 70–81, 110, and 137); a 2nd century group (Nos. 29, 32, 93, 97, 117, and 125) dated by a coin of Hadrian (AD 135) but containing rubbish survivals. [Also published by the National Museum of Wales in a repaginated edition.]

The Roman Amphitheatre at Caerleon, Monmouthshire, by R E M and T V Wheeler, *Archaeologia*, **78** (1928), 111–218. Includes an early 2nd century group (Nos. 2–8, 22–24, 33, 50, 53, 60, 63, and 69), with rubbish survivals; a 3rd century group (Nos. 28, 31, 35, 36, 55, and 56); and a 4th century group (Nos. 18, 20, 21, 27, 30, 66, and 74); as with the preceding, dated much earlier in the report.

The Roman Fort at Brecon, by R E M Wheeler, *Y Cymmrodor*, **37** (1926), 1–260, includes a small mid-2nd century group (fig. 95, C 6–17) from a pit, dated too early in the report; a late 2nd century group (fig. 98, C 33–43) from a drain, dated by samian.

Holt, Denbighshire; The Works-Depôt of the Twentieth Legion at Castle Lyons, by W F Grimes, *Y Cymmrodor*, **41** (1930), 1–235. Includes a useful selection of pottery, mainly 2nd century (figs. 61–76).

The Roman Villa at Llantwit Major in Glamorgan, by V E Nash-Williams, *Archaeol Cambrensis,* **102** (1953), 89–163. Although the report suggests that occupation started in the middle of the 2nd century (p. 129), the evidence of samian and coins indicates a slightly later date. Much of the coarse ware is 4th century (figs. 17–19).

Segontium and the Roman Occupation of Wales, by R E M Wheeler, *Y Cymmrodor*, **33** (1923), 1–186, includes some well stratified 4th century vessels (figs. 77 and 78).

NOTE: Caerleon and the Roman Forts in Wales in the Second Century A.D., by Grace Simpson (*Archaeol Cambrensis*, **111** (1962), 103–66, and **112** (1963), 13–76, reviews the chronologies of most of the excavated forts (published separately as *Britons and the Roman Army*, 1964, Gregg Press).

Drawing pottery

It has now become standard practice to illustrate pottery with an elevation on the right-hand side and a section in solid black on the left. Thus external decoration is shown to the right of a central dividing line and any internal feature to the left. Where, however, an irregular design occurs, the elevation may have to be extended beyond the central line or the decorative motif drawn separately. The full diameter should be shown, but if several vessels of similar type are illustrated it is permissible, after showing one complete vessel, to draw only the sections of the rest, but the diameters should be indicated in the text. All vessels should be drawn full size and mounted on sheets four times the size of the page of text (with an allowance for margins) for the block-maker to reduce them to one-quarter (linear) so that the full sheet then has the dimensions of the page of the text. Very large vessels may be drawn at a reduced scale in the first instance and have a final reduction greater than a quarter. Decorated samian and stamps on mortaria and amphorae are usually reduced by one-half, but other potters' stamps should be full size. There is usually no need to shade the surface of Romano-British vessels or to show variations in surface treatment, as this can be more easily described in the text. The effect of shading is pleasing when done by a skilled draughtsman, but the labour involved is hardly commensurate with the value of the results.

Complete vessels are rarely found and when fragments are drawn there is no need to show the edge of the break unless it cuts across an irregular decorative pattern. A conjectural restoration of the section may be shown by a single dotted line, but this is not normally necessary.

Methods

There are various methods of drawing pottery; only experiments will show which an individual prefers. Ingenious pieces of equipment have been devised to facilitate this process. While these methods are normally simple when the vessels are complete, complications arise with sherds. One method is to set the sherd up in its proper plane with a lump of Plasticine and to take careful vertical and horizontal measurements, plotting them direct on to the drawing. This mechanical method undoubtedly produces accurate results if the sherd is properly set up in the first instance.

1   Measure the outer diameter of the rim wherever possible. This is most easily done by means of a rim-scale. Place the rim upside down on the scale in its proper plane, and check this by looking along the plane of the paper and adjusting the angle at which the sherd is held, until the arc of the rim lies flat on the paper. Then move the rim across the scale until its outer curve coincides exactly with one of the curves on the scale when viewed from above from several positions.

2   Take some paper (preferably squared in faint or blue lines) and draw a horizontal line equal in length to the diameter. Bisect this and draw a perpendicular down from the mid-point.

3   While the sherd is still in position on the rim-scale, measure one or, preferably, two other points on the surface of the vessel. One of these might be on the maximum girth, which may be gauged with the aid of a set-square. Another might be the lowest surviving point of the sherd, which may be measured by use of ruler and set-square together. For both points a vertical measurement from the plane of the rim is also required.

4   Draw the outer profile of the sherd, taking care that it is held in its proper plane to the horizontal line, and in correct relation to the diameter, as set out on the paper. The position should be checked by using a set-square, preferably an engineer's square which stands upright and does not need to be held. When this position has been checked, draw the outline of the sherd by pencil keeping the eye vertically above the point as it moves along the vertical projection of the profile.

5   Either repeat the process for the other profile, or transfer the drawing of the profile to the other side by tracing or by direct plotting if squared paper is being used.

6   Complete the section on the left-hand side by drawing the line of the inside of the vessel. This can be done more accurately by direct measurement than with dividers or calipers. Care must be taken to measure the thickness at right-angles to the body of the sherd, i.e. a radial measurement.

7   Draw an details of decoration—cordons, grooves, etc. Internal details are shown on the left-hand side of the drawing, external ones on the right-hand side.

Details of decoration are drawn in elevation and not perspective, but the curvature of the surface of the sherd will lead to apparent marginal crowding.

This has to be allowed for (as on Fig. 1, No. 6). Horizontal lines are used to define cordons and grooves and other sharp angular changes of direction in the profile. Cordons and grooves may be shown effectively with a slightly thicker line at the top of a groove and the bottom of a cordon.

Examples are shown of methods of representing complicated details of decoration and such features as the spouts of mortaria (No. 21).

When there is an overhanging flange or foot-ring, care should be taken to draw a horizontal line on the section side of the drawing. On the elevation side the corresponding lines eclipses the re-entrant profile, which is not depicted.

8   With the sherd still available for reference, ink the drawing, using a good black Indian or drawing ink, taking care that each line is of consistent thickness. In doing this, it is necessary to consider the size to which the drawings will be reduced, for fine lines may tend to disappear on reduction, and any lines too close together may merge.

Different people prefer different types of pen: individuals will learn only from experience the instrument that suits them best.* A fine brush is useful for inking the section.

9   The drawing should be lightly labelled in pencil with the reference number or other indication of provenance. This will be rubbed out when the final numbering of the figures is co-ordinated with the text. At the same time it is often convenient to write down the description of the fabric and other features considered necessary.

10   It is not, of course, necessary to draw each vessel or sherd in position on the sheet of paper that will be sent to the printer. This only leads to difficulty if mistakes are made. It is easier to draw each vessel separately and to cut the drawing out for mounting later. The paper used for mounting should be chosen carefully, since thin paper warps when gummed. There is some advantage in using squared paper again for mounting, as the lines are useful guides. But again, paper with faint or blue lines is needed.

If a reduction to one-quarter is intended the sheet should be four times the height and width of the space occupied by the printed text on the page of the periodical in which the report is to be published. Do not forget to allow space for the printed caption in these overall measurements. It is convenient to allow a 25 mm margin on each edge of the sheet to facilitate handling and to provide space for writing instructions to the block-maker about the proposed degree of reduction, although blue pencil which is not reproduced on the block can be used on the drawing itself. As periodicals vary in size it is necessary to check these measurements carefully before making up the sheets.

The drawings should be collected together in their groups and laid on the sheets to see how many pages they will occupy. Some juggling may then be necessary to get the best arrangement. If it is impossible to fit them all on to a full page or pages, part of a sheet may be used. Opinion differs on how close drawings may be placed, but with the present high cost of printing an

*A line of suitable thickness can be achieved by using a Rapidograph No. 2 pen, or with a 6 mm stylus.

economical layout which does not appear over-crowded should be the aim. If doubt arises, discussion with the editor may be helpful. The drawings are next pasted on to the sheets, care being taken that they are all correctly aligned to the horizontal. Each drawing should then be numbered. The numbers previously used for identification are unlikely to fit the requirements of the mounted sheets, and a new series running consecutively throughout will be required, using stencils or 'Letraset', Whatever method is used, ambiguity must be avoided and it should be remembered that the letters must be four times the required printed size.

11 An account of the pottery is now needed for the text. This may be done in preliminary form as the drawing proceeds, but the final report usually cannot be completed until the drawings have been mounted and numbered. Vessels should be described in consistent order, e.g.:

a Class or type of vessel.

b Details of form, and condition where significant.

c Fabric

d Decoration.

e Any further points requiring mention, including diameters for vessels drawn only in section.

An example might be:

> Wide-mouthed jar with rim of triangular section in sandy, buff paste with cream slip and traces of burnishing on the body. Decorated on the shoulder with a single wavy line. A hole 5 mm diameter has been bored in the side after firing.

In view of high printing costs, some prefer to omit descriptions of form and decoration when these are obvious from the drawing.

Descriptions of colours are often difficult, and individuals vary greatly in their appreciation of different terms. Colour-charts are not generally helpful, but students are advised to temper their subjective judgments by a judicious use of the *Pottery Colour Chart* prepared for their use by the Study Group for Romano-British Coarse Pottery (available from the CBA or RESCUE, 15A Bull Plain, Hertford).

The search for dated parallels is a necessary part of the preliminary study of the pottery from an excavation, but the space devoted to quoting them in the report will depend upon the quality of the independent dating evidence of a group in its context. Some well dated deposits may need no external support from parallels. Other groups or sherds may have to be dated from evidence already in print; if so, the relevant parallels have to be cited. Care, however, is necessary to ensure that the comparisons are valid, and normally only parallels showing significant identity in form and fabric should be quoted.

12 Finally, all pencil marks and lines should be rubbed out on the drawing, and a check made for errors or ink smudges, which may be concealed with Process White or by pasting paper over them.

Abbreviations used in bibliographical references and publishing organizations

Antiq J	*Antiquaries Journal*, The Society of Antiquaries, London
Archaeologia	The Society of Antiquaries, London
Archaeol Aeliana	*Archaeologia Aeliana*, The Society of Antiquaries, Newcastle-upon-Tyne
Archaeol Cambrensis	*Archaeologia Cambrensis*, The Cambrian Archaeological Association
Archaeol Cantiana	*Archaeologia Cantiana*, The Kent Archaeological Society
Archaeol J	*Archaeological Journal*, The Royal Archaeological Institute
J Roman Stud	*Journal of Roman Studies*, The Society for the Promotion of Roman Studies
Norfolk Archaeol	*Norfolk Archaeology*, The Norfolk and Norwich Archaeological Society
Proc Prehist Soc	*Proceedings of the Prehistoric Society*
RCHM	Royal Commission on Historical Monuments
VCH	*Victoria County History*
Y Cymmrodor	*Transactions* of the Honourable Society of Cymmrodorion

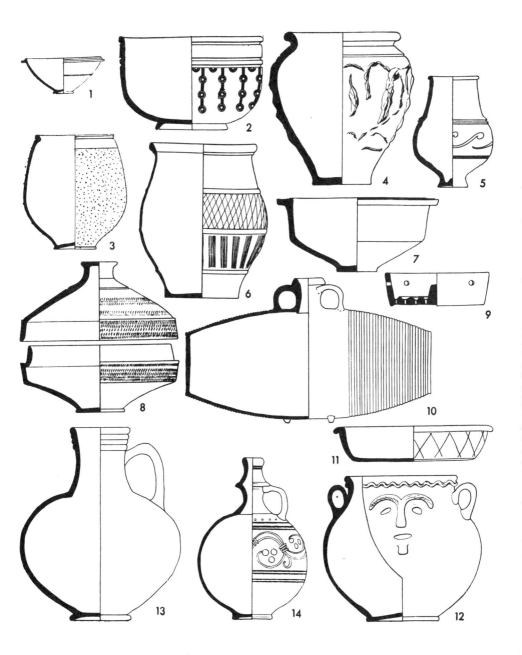

Fig. 1. Examples of types of vessel and decoration ($\frac{1}{4}$)

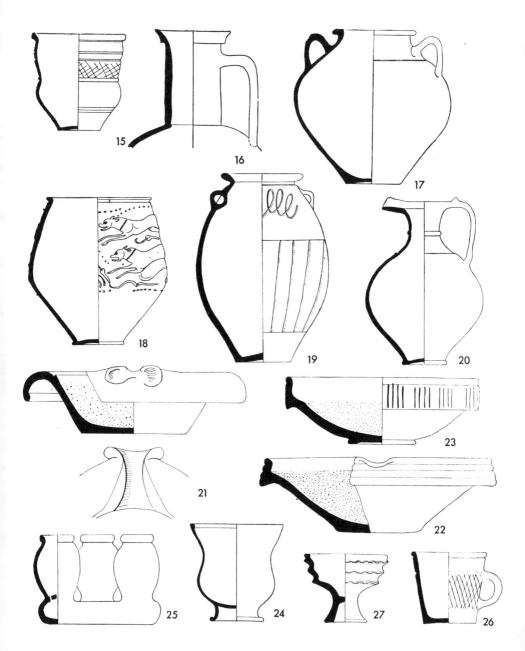

Fig. 2. Examples of types of vessel and decoration $(\frac{1}{4})$

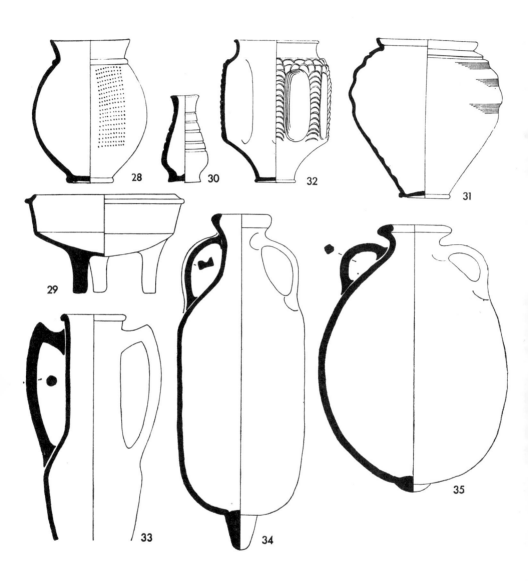

Fig. 3. Examples of types of vessel and decoration ($\frac{1}{4}$; except Nos. 33-35, $\frac{1}{8}$)